OXFORD

The City & University

MICHAEL WATTS

FRONT COVER: *The Danby Gateway to the Botanical Garden, given to the University by the Earl of Danby in 1621. In the background is the tower of Magdalen College, completed in 1509.*

BACK COVER: *Situated at the junction of two rivers, Oxford offers ample opportunities for undergraduates and visitors to relax while being punted about by energetic and willing friends.*

RIGHT: *Tom Tower, Christ Church, completed by Sir Christopher Wren, near the site of a former medieval church demolished by Cardinal Wolsey when he began to build the College.*

Although the first reference to Oxford is to be found in the *Anglo-Saxon Chronicle* in A.D. 912, it is reasonable to suppose that this important site had been occupied and developed for some considerable time before the 10th century. Its geographical location near the junction of the Rivers Thames and Cherwell made settlement here almost inevitable. Low-lying and unhealthy it may have been, but in the Anglo-Saxon political situation few could have missed its strategic importance, for all that the Romans had chosen virtually to ignore the area during their occupation.

Its early history is obscure and only fitfully evidenced, but slowly it developed to have become a place of some considerable significance by the time of the Norman Conquest. One historian has said that in the fifty years preceding the Conquest Oxford saw more of the English kings and their followers than at any other time in its history.

The city continued to develop during the 12th century, and then there is evidence of the beginning of a decline. The most recent opinion is that the extent to which de-urbanisation took place can be appreciated visually in the garden of Merton College, which is on the site of ten or twelve deserted houses, and in the vast area covered by New College, the site of which, acquired in 1370, was formerly occupied by more than 30 houses. It seems possible that, but for the fortuitous arrival of the scholars, Oxford would have continued to decline.

It is difficult to be certain why the University was established at Oxford and not elsewhere. A variety of factors played their part. There was a site where property was cheaply and readily available. The place was far removed from the centre of the political life of the country and as far as possible from the long arm of the local ecclesiastical authority vested in the Bishop of Lincoln, in whose diocese Oxford was situated at that time. The city was readily accessible from all

parts of southern and western England and contact with the continent was relatively easy via Southampton and Bristol. This last was important until 1167, when, for political reasons, Henry II made it virtually impossible for Englishmen to study at the University of Paris. Perhaps this royal veto, more than anything else, led to the growth of the University at Oxford. Already there had been passing references to scholars and lectures at Oxford—Theobald of Étampes and the Lombard lawyer Vacarius—but from the middle of the 12th century the body of scholars at Oxford appears to have increased rapidly in number.

What sort of men came to study here at the time? In the *Canterbury Tales* Chaucer has left us a graphic account of the fictional, nocturnal escapades of the sweet-voiced, gallant scholar in the *Miller's Tale* and of two others, albeit Cambridge men, in the *Reeve's Tale,* but he has taken care to balance matters with an equally telling description of the Oxford Clerk, too unworldly to seek for secular employment, whose prime care was study, whose speech was filled with moral virtue, avid for learning and equally eager to impart knowledge whenever the opportunity was afforded. Such men were not the gilded youths whose future place in society was predetermined or assured. The students were often the cleverest sons of middle-class families who left their homes, took minor Orders and came to the University as the first step along the path of professional and social advancement. It was the only way open to high preferment in the Church and therefore in the political life of the country at this time for those not born into the ruling class. An example of

★

ABOVE: *In the foreground, the Sheldonian Theatre and the Clarendon Building. In the background, All Souls, the Schools Quadrangle, the Radcliffe Camera, the University Church and Christ Church Cathedral.*

such a career would be that of Thomas Wolsey, who came to Magdalen College from Ipswich, where his father was a butcher, and rose to be the most powerful person at the court of King Henry VIII during the early years of his reign. "All who aspired to rise by their wits to be civil servants, secretaries of great men, physicians, architects or ecclesiastical lawyers, must needs take Holy Orders and pass through the University."

As in the early days of a marriage there are often periods of strain and outright disagreement as the two parties learn to adjust to one another, so it was in the development of the relationship between the University and the City, and from time to time matters erupted into violence and bloodshed. The townsmen often exploited the needs of the scholars. Short measure was given in the market-place and extortionate prices were charged. There is equally clear evidence of provocative behaviour on the part of the scholars, or at least of some of them. In 1209 the provocation was accidental in as far as there does not appear to have been any intention of killing the townswoman in revenge for whose death the citizens summarily killed three innocent students. In the face of lynch law the other scholars speedily fled the town, some making for the eastern fen lands to settle at Cambridge and establish the nucleus of the University there. It took a long time to sort matters out and it was only after four years that the academic community resumed its settled existence at Oxford. The settlement, like all subsequent ones after disputes between Town and Gown, was clearly to the advantage of the University. Nearly every dispute was settled in such a way as to add to their privileges, so that by the middle of the 15th century "the town had been crushed and was almost entirely subjugated to the authority of the University. The burghers lived henceforth in their own town almost as helots or subjects of a conquering people."

The most memorable clash between the University and the City came in the great riot of St Scholastica's Day in February 1355. A squabble between some members of the University and a tavernkeeper developed so as eventually to involve the whole town. The citizens rallied to the call of the bell of the City church of St Martin at Carfax, while the scholars responded to the rival tolling of the bell of the University Church in the High Street. The stretch of roadway between these two churches was the traditional battlefield between the two factions and one University historian has remarked that "there is probably not a single yard of ground in any part of the classic High Street between St Martin's and St Mary's which has not at some time or another been stained with blood. There are historic battlefields on which less has been spilt." The townsfolk were assisted by insurgent forces from the outlying villages in a high passion of anti-clerical fervour. Inns and Halls were plundered and fired, the scholars' books were destroyed. Even the churches could not afford their customary sanctuary to the outnumbered students who, quite reasonably, fled the town, returning only when a general pardon for the clerks had been issued. Even then, four months later we hear of Edward III's plea to the masters to resume their lectures and get the University back to normal working. It was only natural that he should be concerned at such a lengthy disruption in the education of a valued and important part of the Civil Service. After all, diplomatic relations with France were such that the young men could hardly transfer to Paris to complete their education!

When the students began to settle in Oxford in the 12th century they lived as they could, lodging in inns and with townsfolk, or, grouping themselves together, some would rent a house for their exclusive use. They had come simply to be members of the University; there were no colleges to which to come. The arrival of the Friars in the 13th century, part of a great wave of foreign influences which had been sweeping into Britain in the wake of the Norman Conquest, was to enhance further the reputation of the young University. It has been suggested that the large Oxford priories, in double-edged fashion, may have given some impetus to the founding of the Colleges. The argument about which College was established first will never be resolved, such are the niceties of interpretation involved. Balliol was

*

FACING PAGE, above: *Oriel College, 'The House of the Blessed Virgin Mary in Oxford', to give it its full style. It was founded by Edward II, one of the two figures in the niches over the steps leading up to the Hall. The other is Charles I.*

FACING PAGE, below: *University College; the gateway to the Radcliffe Quadrangle. For a long time it was held that the College was founded by King Alfred, and this view was upheld in the Law Courts as late as 1727. In fact its statutes date from 1280.*

RIGHT: *The University Church of St Mary the Virgin, the third church to stand on this site. Formerly used as a library, treasury, meeting-place and court-house, it was also the scene of the formal academic disputations and the place in which degrees were conferred.*

ABOVE: *The Library, Queen's College. The college, founded in 1341, has been totally transformed architecturally. The process began in the last quarter of the 17th century and this Library was built 1692–5, possibly to the design of Dean Aldrich of Christ Church. The spacious 18th-century architecture makes it outstanding among the colleges of both Oxford and Cambridge.*

LEFT: *New College Chapel. The present reredos dates from 1888. The glass in the choir is 18th century, that in the Ante Chapel 14th century. The Founder's crosier is encased on the north wall of the Choir. Nearby is El Greco's painting of St James, given in 1961. The West window is from cartoons by Sir Joshua Reynolds.*

FACING PAGE: *Merton College. It was only gradually that these buildings assumed the familiar form of an Oxford Quadrangle. Mob Quad is the result of a gradual accumulation of buildings and not deliberate design. This accidental formation was deliberately adopted by the Founder of New College, whose buildings served as a model for all later large foundations.*

founded in 1263 as a penance imposed by the Bishop of Durham. University College had received its original endowment in 1249, but it is claimed that Merton College was the first to achieve true collegiate existence, being founded shortly before Balliol by Walter de Merton, sometime Chancellor of England. Exeter (1314), Oriel (1326) and Queen's College (1341) followed. The founding of New College (1379) by William of Wykeham, Bishop of Winchester, set a pattern to be followed by all subsequent foundations, although half a century was to elapse before the founding of the next College, Lincoln (1427), in reaction to and as a bastion against the Wycliffite teachings which had been disturbing the University. Wykeham was the first founder to conceive the idea of making a college not merely an endowed lodging-house for students, "but a house of community which could vie in the splendour of its buildings and the dignity of its corporate life with the great capitular and monastic establishments" and he associated it with his school at Winchester, the first English Public School. Whereas all colleges previously had admitted only graduates, Wykeham made provision for the education of young men who had yet to graduate and Wayneflete extended the principle when he established Magdalen (1448). Shortly before Wayneflete founded what many look upon as the most beautiful of the Oxford colleges, Archbishop Chichele had founded All Souls (1438) placing a special emphasis on the study of Canon and Civil Law in the allocation of Fellowships there. In true medieval fashion it was to be a house of prayer as well as of study. Henry VI in granting the charter said that prayer should be made both for the King and for the Archbishop "while alive and for our souls when we shall have migrated from this light, as well as for the souls of the most illustrious Prince Henry, late King of England, of Thomas, late Duke of Clarence our uncle, of the Dukes, Barons, Knights, Esquires and other noble subjects of our father and ourself, who in the times and under the command of our father and ourself, fell in the wars for the crown of France, and for the souls of all the faithful departed." To this day it remains a college with no undergraduate body, a reminder in times when junior members clamour for representation on Governing Bodies that there was a period when they figured far less prominently in the life of Colleges than the provisions of the State have enabled them to do in the latter half of the 20th century.

In the founding charter of Brasenose College (1509) there was little to indicate any impact being made by the intellectual ferment of the Renaissance, but the charter of Corpus Christi College (1517) gives clear signs of the changes. Founded by Bishop Fox of Winchester, a distinguished statesman who drew Wolsey into political life, it was intended to be no "monkish" college but a place of liberal education such as had been unknown hitherto in Oxford. The study of theology still figured most prominently, but it was to be grounded in the study of the Ancient Fathers rather than pursued along the customary medieval lines. Provision was made for the teaching of Greek as well as Latin, and for this reason alone Erasmus was prepared to say that it would be "one of the chief glories of Britain."

Eight years later the foundation stone was laid of the largest of Oxford's colleges, known first as Cardinal College, but now as Christ Church. Having suppressed the Priory of St Frideswide, Cardinal Wolsey proposed to build on the site a college which a contemporary foresaw was designed "to excel, not only all other colleges, but even the palaces of princes." The provision in the original

statutes was for a grandiose foundation, but when Wolsey fell from power his unfinished college was forfeit to the Crown. In 1532 the king established a new college on the site and renamed it King Henry VIII's College but it survived only until 1545 and in the following year the king established Christ Church, uniting the Cathedral of the newly founded See of Oxford with the College. It was to be a cathedral and college in one, not two institutions existing side by side, but a place like All Souls with a dual function. There it had been college and chantry, here it was to be college and cathedral, a thoroughly medieval arrangement which has persisted down to the present day, despite all the other changes which have taken place in Church and State. The college remained as Wolsey left it for nearly a hundred years. Tom Tower was completed by Sir Christopher Wren, but the arches round Tom Quad remind the visitor of Wolsey's unfulfilled plans for the cloistered walk of a different college from that which now exists.

The founding of Trinity College (1555), St John's College (1555) and Jesus College (1571) mark the culmination of this remarkable period of development in the University. They also point to the rise of a type of founder hitherto unknown. Trinity College was founded by Sir Thomas Pope and a few weeks later St John's College was founded by Sir Thomas White. Both colleges owe their origin to men who had grown rich in the social and economic changes brought about by the rise of the Tudors. Pope was a friend of Sir Thomas More who nevertheless found it possible, and to

*

LEFT: *The tower and cloister of Magdalen College, founded by Wayneflete, Bishop of Winchester, who was given licence to found Magdalen Hall for the study of Theology and Philosophy. Later he was given the Hospital of St John Baptist outside the East Gate. Both were absorbed in Magdalen College.*

FACING PAGE: *The Chapel Screen, All Souls College, one of the most pleasing of all Oxford College Chapels. The Screen dates from the 17th century but was remodelled in 1716. The restored reredos dominates the East end. (All the figures are 19th century.) The medieval glass is particularly noteworthy.*

his advantage, to work with Thomas Cromwell. Like many others he secured properties at the dissolution of the monasteries—30 manors which had once been in monastic hands—and in consequence became a great Oxfordshire landowner. Like Pope, the founder of St John's College, a merchant tailor, was a devoted supporter of the old religion and established his college "to strengthen the orthodox faith in so far as it is weakened by the damage of time and the malice of men." By the time that Jesus College was founded—nominally by Elizabeth I, in fact by the Treasurer of St David's Cathedral if the honour is given to the person who endows the foundation—it was possible to dedicate a college to the pursuit of true religion, meaning by that term the reformed version of it, thus giving the college the distinction of being the first Protestant college in Oxford.

In the years which separate the founding of Cardinal College and Jesus College, England had agonised its way through the upheaval of the Reformation and few could have expected the University to get off so easily as it did in the process, bearing in mind the very close ties between the University and the Church which had existed ever since its establishment three centuries earlier. "No institutions depended more than the Universities upon the Church. None owed more to the special jurisdiction and the privileged immunities which the clergy had secured. None had more to fear from anti-clerical reaction." The University had to contend with an official Visitation by men who had little sympathy, if any, with the old system of education, and then later the full impact of the dissolution of the monasteries was felt. The Friars who had contributed so much to the life of the medieval University disappeared and the fate of the monasteries at Canterbury, Durham and Gloucester was inevitably reflected in the colleges which they had established at Oxford. In all this uncertainty Henry VIII gave several assurances to the University about its future, but when he died and was succeeded by Edward VI, all the former fears returned, for the new reign meant the triumph of Reformation principles, and Protestants in the University came to the fore. Further Visitations ensued and religious tests, a device which was to be the source of endless trouble in the future, were introduced. With the accession of Mary everything went into reverse and the Protestants fled to the security of the Continent. The Mass was heard again and vestments which had been hidden away reappeared. The most notable event of the time in Oxford was the trial and execution of

★

FACING PAGE, above: *The Dining Hall of Brasenose College, which is often referred to as BNC. It takes its name from the door knocker of the Hall which formerly occupied the site. A Brazen Nose can be seen on the panelling behind the High Table.*

FACING PAGE, below: *Corpus Christi College. The sundial in the middle of the paved quadrangle was erected in 1581. A perpetual calendar was added in 1606. It did not lose its plate in the Civil War and in consequence possesses priceless domestic and ecclesiastical silver-gilt pieces.*

ABOVE RIGHT: *Trinity College Chapel, rebuilt 1691–4 to replace an earlier building which had fallen into decay. Designed by Dean Aldrich of Christ Church, possibly advised by Wren. The woodwork is thought to be by Grinling Gibbons, the painted ceiling by Pierre Berchet.*

ABOVE: *Pembroke College Chapel, built in 1728, was "enriched and beautified" by C. E. Kempe in 1884. Dr Samuel Johnson was at this college for 14 months and the library contains some of his manuscripts.*

FACING PAGE: *Christ Church Cathedral; formerly St Frideswide's Priory, it became both College Chapel and Cathedral Church of the newly formed diocese of Oxford, carved out of the medieval diocese of Lincoln in 1546.*

Archbishop Cranmer and Bishops Latimer and Ridley. They were brought to Oxford to defend their beliefs and statements about the Eucharist in 1554, languishing in prison for eighteen months after their initial disputation. In September 1555 their trial was opened at the University Church. Within a month their opinions had been condemned and Latimer and Ridley were burned at the stake opposite Balliol College. Cranmer followed them some months later, having made a dramatically defiant and unexpected statement of his beliefs in St Mary's Church before being hustled off to his death.

With the accession of Elizabeth I things headed for change once more, but not over-speedily. For the University it was a period of adaptation rather than dramatic change.

Only two colleges were founded while the Stuarts were kings of England. Early in the reign of James I, Nicholas Wadham, a well known west-country landowner, founded the college which bears his name, built on the site of a former Augustinian Priory. In 1624 Pembroke College was founded in the former Broadgates Hall, taking its name from the Chancellor of the University at the time, the Earl of Pembroke. After this there was a lull in founding colleges but building went on apace in those which existed already, and in the University as far as political circumstances and the economy permitted.

The University's first library had been built in the 14th century at the Church of St Mary the Virgin which was then the centre of the life of the young University. In the 15th century Humfrey, Duke of Gloucester, had given the University a valuable collection of manuscripts which was housed in space provided over the Divinity School, which was being built at that time. That library was subsequently dispersed and in 1598, retiring from politics, Sir Thomas Bodley decided to devote the remainder of his life to re-establishing the University Library, contributing considerably to the project himself. The restored Library was formally opened in 1602 but quickly it became necessary to provide more library space and the building of the Schools Quadrangle was seized as an opportunity to do this after the addition of the Arts End in 1612.

For a long time there had been growing unease about the continued use of the University Church for secular occasions as well as for services. After the Restoration the Sheldonian Theatre was built to provide an assembly room for the University. It was the gift of Sheldon, Archbishop of Canterbury, and was the first architectural commission given to the young Christopher Wren, then Professor of Astronomy in the University. The Clarendon building (1713) which stands close to the Sheldonian was originally the home of the University Press and was built with the proceeds from the sale of the Earl of Clarendon's account of that Civil War which made such a marked impact on Oxford in the 17th century.

During the Civil War the University was predominantly royalist, as might have been expected, and the king, quitting London, brought his Court here, living in Christ Church himself,

★

LEFT: *The Divinity School — the oldest lecture room in Oxford, built during the 15th century for the teaching of Theology. The progress of the building was hampered for lack of funds and took 60 years to complete. The vaulting is a show-piece of Gothic architecture and may have been designed by William Orchard (d.1504), a leading Oxford master mason.*

his queen nearby at Merton College. Loyally the University and individual colleges handed over money and plate to the Royal Exchequer to finance the king's stand against Parliament, preparing themselves enthusiastically at the same time for the struggle which they saw must inevitably ensue. Ultimately it was to no avail. Oxford surrendered to the Parliamentary forces and the king was forced to flee from the city disguised as a servant. From then on until the Restoration in 1660 the life of the University was sadly disrupted. A policy of passive resistance to the Parliamentary power was adopted. Some royalists fled and Cromwell's nominees were intruded on unwilling colleges. In such a situation it is surprising that even small oases of scholarship flourished, but there is plenty of evidence that scholarly activity was not wholly abandoned. After the years of disturbance and unsettlement it is small wonder that the news of the Restoration was received with such wild enthusiasm.

It is customary to describe the next 150 years of University life as a period of decline and decay, and there is evidence to support the statement. Gibbon, looking back to the short time he spent at Magdalen College, wrote: "The Fellows of my time were decent, easy men, who supinely enjoyed the gifts of the founder. From the toil of reading or thinking or writing they had absolved their conscience, and the first shoots of learning and ingenuity withered on the ground without yielding any fruit." Later he found that there were more heartening signs in another college and told his readers that "Under the auspices of late Deans, a more regular discipline has been introduced at Christ Church. Learning has been made a duty, a pleasure and even a fashion." Despite that, statistics show that there was a fall in the number of men wishing to come to the University, and a pronounced feature of the period was the decline in the admission of the children of the nobility and the gentry, Oxford seemingly no longer providing the training which a man of quality wanted for his offspring.

If only one College was founded in the 18th century—Worcester (1714)—the face of Oxford was changed in many other ways. Significant alterations were made to the existing buildings at Queen's, All Souls, Christ Church and Magdalen and vestigial remains of medieval Oxford—the North Gate of the City and the Bocardo Prison—were removed. There was even talk of replacing the University Church with a building in the classical style!

By the end of the 18th century there was mounting criticism of University life both from outside and from within the University itself. Of course, to some, perhaps a majority at first, the idea of reform of any sort was abhorrent, but as the 19th century wore on the case for change became more and more evident and battle was joined. What it amounted to was that two theories of the purpose of University education were in conflict. "For centuries Oxford had been the cradle of the Church of England. Education was in the hands of its clergy, who held almost all Fellowships and generally

*

RIGHT: *The Convocation House at the west end of the Divinity School, built 1634–7, where the business of the University was formerly transacted. The National Parliament met here several times when driven from London by the Plague. The fan-vaulting was put in during the 18th century. Nearby is the Chancellor's Court where cases affecting members of the University were tried.*

looked to a career in the Church on leaving the University, and admission was restricted to Anglicans. In such a system, education was not vocational, except for the clergy, and more attention was paid to the training of judgement and to the inculcation of Christian morals than to the advancement of learning. Yet within a few years the monopoly of the Church of England had been fatally breached and by a succession of Acts of Parliament commencing with the Oxford Act of 1854, the University was liberalised, ancient restrictions removed and the principle of free competition established. The University became increasingly secular in character, the gradual abolition of tests and oaths opened it to those sections of the community previously excluded and learning was stimulated by opening Fellowships and increasing the professoriate."

In such a situation the founding of Keble College in 1870 was warmly welcomed by some, in as far as it was planned to run the college in such a way as to enable men who had hitherto been unable to afford university education to be admitted. But it was viewed with suspicion by others who saw it as designed to perpetuate the very underlying religious attitudes which had been so vigorously opposed and attacked by the reforming, liberal

*

ABOVE LEFT: *St Catherine's College, founded 1962, designed by Arne Jacobsen who was responsible not only for the buildings but also for the gardens, the furniture and the college plate. The work was financed by industry, commerce, private benefactors and charitable foundations.*

BELOW LEFT: *St Anne's College, incorporated 1952, is another modern college to which a number of architects have made their contribution. The mural illustrated here is by Stefan Kapp.*

FACING PAGE, above: *St Edmund Hall, the only medieval Hall to survive to our own day. Lately it has expanded considerably and the nearby church of St Peter-in-the-East is now used as a College library.*

FACING PAGE, below: *Nuffield College (1937) exists to encourage research in social studies by making easier the cooperation of academic and non-academic persons. It was the first college to admit both men and women.*

spirits in the University. Named after John Keble, a leading figure in the Oxford movement in the early part of the 19th century, it was generously supported by those who wished to see the Christian and more particularly the Anglican tradition upheld in the University, and opposed by those who saw the Church's position as one which made for illiberal attitudes and an obscurantism which should have no place in a modern educational establishment.

In the hundred years which have elapsed since the completion of the 19th-century reform of the University, two developments of outstanding significance have affected the character of the University: the admission of women, with the consequent founding and growth of the women's Colleges; and the increasingly important place accorded to scientific studies in the curricula, bringing in its wake the development of the Science Area, which has enabled modern architects to add their substantial contribution to the Oxford skyline.

Perhaps nothing has moved at greater speed than the development of women's education, starting with the formation of an Association for the Higher Education of Women at Oxford in 1878, and the subsequent establishment of two halls of residence, Lady Margaret Hall, restricted to Anglicans, and Somerville, without any restriction in membership. Seven years later St Hugh's and in 1893 St Hilda's came into being. In 1879 the Society of Oxford Home Students, which was to become St Anne's College in 1952, had been established. Male chauvinism provided a vociferous and predictable resistance. It was felt that there was something indelicate, if not dangerous, in allowing some of the nation's future mothers to read and study unrestrictedly! The ageing Dr Pusey, Canon of Christ Church, viewed the whole movement with great alarm and accounted it one of the greatest misfortunes to afflict the University—and he would claim to have survived many during his long lifetime. There was a certain illogicality, however, in allowing the young ladies, properly chaperoned, to attend lectures and sit examinations, but not allowing them to receive degrees. This state of affairs was not remedied until 1920 and in respect of degrees in Theology not until 1935! Now further steps have been taken and many colleges have altered their statutes to

allow them to admit women to these hitherto exclusively male preserves.

Two world wars and an unprecedented pace of social change have transformed Oxford. Gone are such things as compulsory attendance at Chapel; gate hours have become almost a thing of the past, and the undergraduates come and go with a freedom at which even their fathers marvel when they recall the more restricted existence they led here immediately after World War II. Administrative reform also has been a feature of the period, viewed with suspicion in some quarters by people fearing for the independence of the colleges in the increasingly centralising processes of University administration. There are still those around who would sympathise with the point of view expressed by Lord Hugh Cecil—"Reform the University! You may as well reform a cheese—there is a certain flavour about a University as there is about a cheese, springing from its antiquity, which may very easily be lost by mishandling." Oxford has been lucky so far. It has not lost its distinctive character despite all the changes.

Throughout their history the colleges have depended heavily upon the loyal and affectionate service of successive generations of townsfolk, for all that official relations between Town and Gown have been strained to breaking-point at times. In a corner of the cloisters at Christ Church there is a memorial tablet, erected in 1787, in

★

FACING PAGE and ABOVE RIGHT: *The Sheldonian Theatre, given to the University by Gilbert Sheldon, Archbishop of Canterbury. The architect was the young Christopher Wren who had little practical experience of building at the time. Wren's roof was rebuilt in 1802 and an overlarge cupola replaced his original work in 1838. The building was restored 1959–60. The painted ceiling* — Truth descending upon the Arts and Sciences — *the work of Robert Streater, Serjeant Painter to the King, was executed in his Whitehall studio.*

BELOW RIGHT: *The Chancellor, together with the Proctors, the Heads of Houses and the Doctors of the University in procession to the Sheldonian Theatre to confer Honorary Degrees at Encaenia, having previously partaken of Lord Crewe's benefaction — strawberries and champagne — at the college of the Vice-Chancellor.*

ABOVE: *One of the many galleries of the Ashmolean Museum.*

LEFT: *Also in the Ashmolean, a section of Uccello's* "A Hunt in a Forest". *The museum houses one of the finest collections of Michaelangelo and Raphael drawings, a famous collection of musical instruments and a collection of coins second only to that in the British Museum. A whole department is devoted to Eastern art and among the British antiquities is the King Alfred Jewel. A room is devoted to the works of the Pre-Raphaelites.*

FACING PAGE: *The Bodleian Library, founded originally by Humfrey, Duke of Gloucester,* c. *1445 and refounded by Thomas Bodley in 1598 after its dispersal in the reign of Edward VI. He arranged with the Stationers' Company which controlled the output of books that they would send the library a free copy of every book printed in England. It now houses over 2,000,000 volumes.*

front of which visitors are often to be seen reading and smiling wryly to themselves. It commemorates one William Pound, a college porter who, "by an exemplary life and behaviour and an honest attention to the duties of his station deserved and obtained the approbation and esteem of the whole society." To William Pound and his like, colleges and successive generations of undergraduates freely admit that they owe an incalculable debt for the contribution which they have made to the life of the place. Now sons no longer follow fathers in the service of a college, having been lured away by the attraction of the wages offered in the nearby car industry or at Pressed Steel. For the first time in its history the University has ceased to be the major employer in Oxford. It resisted all efforts to introduce light industry to Oxford, but Cowley developed so quickly and almost unexpectedly that there was little if anything that the University could do, even if it had wanted to. William Morris, later Lord Nuffield, possibly Oxford's most generous benefactor, working from very small beginnings developed a car industry here which transformed the City of Oxford in a way which can be compared only with the long-term effects of the arrival of the scholars nearly 800 years before. In doing this he gave the citizens a degree of independence in the matter of choice of employment which had not been available to their predecessors, and that cannot but be a good thing, however inconvenient for College Domestic Bursars!

Inevitably in this brief summary of the history of the City and University, reference has been in the main to events which have been etched deeply on the public memory, but for everyone who has ever been to Oxford, either as an undergraduate or simply as a visitor walking round its medieval colleges, all that, if remembered at all, is overlaid with a host of personal memories which provides them with their own particular picture of Oxford—May morning revels, a College Ball, punting on the river, hours of idle chatter in a coffee shop, talk far into the night about politics or ethics or whatever comes to mind, Evensong on a winter's day in the Cathedral, the Deer Park at Magdalen, cricket in the Parks, the galleries of the Ashmolean, a performance of the B minor Mass in the Sheldonian, Eights Week races on the river—the list is endless. It is from such things that the image is formed which the visitor carries away fixed ineradicably in his memory, of a city to which, like the other great centres of European civilisation, he returns again and again with pleasure and ever deepening affection.

★

ABOVE LEFT: *Broad Street. Here we see four of the "Emperors' Heads" (restored 1974) outside the Sheldonian Theatre. There are those who think they are the Apostles or ancient philosophers!*

ABOVE RIGHT: *The Martyrs' Memorial, 1841, designed by Scott and erected by evangelicals in the heat of the Oxford Movement to commemorate the "Protestant martyrs," Cranmer, Latimer and Ridley.*

FACING PAGE: *The Radcliffe Camera. Designed by James Gibbs, this is the finest example of a circular library in England. In 1863 the lower arches were glazed and a new entrance provided to make an additional reading room.*

ABOVE: *Eights Week is an invariable part of Oxford's timetable in Trinity Term. Eight-oared racing started at Eton and began at Oxford in 1815. The college boats set off at equal intervals along the river and the object of the race is to catch up with the boat immediately in front and to bump its stern. The college whose boat is first over the finishing line in the final race, having not been "bumped", is declared "Head of the River" for that year.*

LEFT: *St Giles's Fair. "It is an inexorable sort of festivity. The whole wide street of St Giles is closed for it. Traffic is diverted, business is disrupted, and all among the plane trees there proliferate the side shows, caravans and pulsing generators of the showmen. It is the most boisterous of Oxford traditions, the profits of which go partly to the city and partly to the college of St John's, the local landowner." (James Morris: Oxford; quoted by kind permission of Faber & Faber Ltd.)*

SBN 85372 049 5